PATIENCE & TAPE

A COLLECTION OF SHORT STORIES

BY LOVANDA BROWN

Patience & Tape
© Lovanda Brown LLC 2019
ISBN 978-0-578-61176-1

Dedication

Thank you, God, for allowing me to grow through the most challenging year of my life. To endure loss is both a humbling and visceral experience. I'm blessed to have endured it with you.

And to Gramma Gwenny—your story deserves a space all its own. The world will know you in due time. What a day when such luck meets the world. I love you.

Table of Contents

DEDICATION 2

SILENCE 5

MRS. BROWN 23

TEARS 47

SUB-MOM CAROL 80

SURVIVING THE CHOKEHOLD 118

I STILL REMEMBER 126

JASON..131

AWAKE 136

BLAINE...148

SELF-LOATHING RANT 151

ABOUT LAST NIGHT 154

8 A.M..160

Silence

Outside, distant sirens and screeching tires darted down the road. The loud demand filled the silence for a few moments, and its whirring refrain lingered in their ears for some time. Finally, the ringing dissolved and it appeared the silence was back. The cream-smeared walls held up the wooden clock, and its glass face grimaced with a crooked smile. The smile read 8:15, and its thin, overlooked hand was ready to perform again. The hand danced rhythmically *tick, tock, tick, tock,* disrupting the silence once more.

Occasionally they would look up from the long dinner table that extended between them and listen carefully to ambulance alerts and kinked engines. The table was empty now with the exception of the pair, but still they sat. The children had gone off to bed and the tension had rushed the wise grandmother off to bed just the same. Just an hour before, thunderous sounds of clicking and clinking filled the air. Forks to plate, glasses to table and of course the occasional phlegm loosening "ahem" were among the topics of conversation. Now, the two sat in a heavy, unspoken quarrel—a silent dispute all too real.

Connor Blake sat and contemplated the ennui his life had become, and it seemed almost every disagreement he had with Grace stemmed from that. As he sat slouched in his chair, he watched the perspiring cup before him. The ice was melting, and he knew he would need another pour. His long lanky legs sprawled out underneath the table, and his circular frames rested on the place setting right next to the half-eaten meal his wife prepared just hours before. Small spheres of Brussel sprouts and well-done steak remained on his plate, opposite of him were the remains of Grace's dinner and the scents gathered to meet the thick tension. He couldn't help but remember the many silent conversations held between his parents. He'd stand in the shadows of the night and watch them stare at each other from across the family table. His father usually held a hard expression; his mother was usually flustered. He couldn't understand how they could sit like that for hours, wake up the next morning and diligently tend to their routines. The thought was broken.

"Why can't we--"

"Please, just don't say anything right now," he said interrupting her.

"But I just thought we should talk about this."

"And we will. Just please, stop talking. I can't hear myself think."

Grace remembers just last night he told her they would, "discuss it in the morning." The sun rose and so did the children. Along with his morning coffee and worn briefcase, he carried half the discussion with him to work while she waited at home. Now they sat together in the home they built together, and she couldn't shake the fact that she missed him. He was sitting right before her and she missed him deeply. She couldn't help but remember when communication was all they had.

She missed the conversations about nothing and the passionate fights about everything. She sat both pale and flustered, a look he had grown accustomed to. Even her brown curls that he once loved were bereft of color. Her once plum cheeks had thinned noticeably and hugged the bones her face carried underneath. Her sullen eyes watched him. With even lips pursed together in a flat line, she watched his body communicate all the things his voice couldn't seem to utter.

He buried his face in hands and let out a loud sigh. She tousled her brown hair from one side to the next with one palm and crossed both arms before her chest. Still nothing was said. The clock held a consistent conversation with itself.

"Tick"

"Tock"

"Tick"

"Tock"

As did the leaky faucet, but still you had two people, who couldn't even muster the same monosyllabic conversation as one held by an inanimate clock. They used to be in love.

"Why won't he talk to her?" said a thought emerging from the night to join the crowded silence.

He was just ten years old, but he knew what happiness looked like. His thin fingers wrapped around the outline of the family room's entrance, and his body held place behind the masking wall. He was tall and lanky for his age. He removed his circular glasses from its resting place above his nose and gently caressed each lens with his shirt. He placed them back on and let one eye meet the silent scene. They used to be happy. He remembered that. It displayed all over the house. The wedding photos and Christmas portraits were once ignored by the young boy. Now, he would give anything just to see them smile like that again. He couldn't understand how they could sit for hours like that at night, and still manage to get him ready for school in the morning. He couldn't understand why they just couldn't talk.

Was it a game? No, of course not. That's the same expression his mother had when she was called to meet with his principal. The disappointed demeanor was harsher than the punishment.

The stern gaze never lifted from his father's blue eyes, but his mother's pained stare broke his heart. She was hurt and he knew it.

"Listen, you said you wanted to talk about this," Grace said.

"I know that's what I said, but--" he stopped right there. He wanted to tell her everything-- that he was tired of his mediocre life, that the disdain for it was quite frankly abysmal and he wasn't sure how to fix that.

But the words would only stain the silence. No more silent conversations and tending to routines to avoid these feelings. Words would only pierce the practice of seeming happy. He wasn't sure they could bounce back from that. Some things were just better left unsaid, he supposed. They'd get back to where they were. He needed time to figure out all he would say, but mostly, all he wouldn't.

Looking down the hole of the now empty glass, he couldn't bring himself to stain the silence, so he embraced it awhile longer.

And somehow, understanding just what he meant, his wife leaned back, sipped from her glass and resolved to share the moment with him.

Mrs. Brown

Her calloused palms graze down the "Jamaica" stamped apron as she smooth wrinkles blended in with curry stains. She is a proud, short, and robust woman, though the pride of her figure varies between each meal. "You know seh mi a get too roun'? Mi need fi tek off some weight," she admits after finishing her grease filled meal. That's always how the stories start.

"Bwoy, mi memba when mi did nice an slim and trim," she begins in broken English that is unrecognizable to the untrained air. Her voice is aged and strong, even grainy and loud—the result of scolding her seven children for years.

She was born in Westmoreland, Jamaica on a rocky road simply called *Orange Hill*.

Small stone houses and trees replete with oranges and mangoes outlined the path leading up to her home on the hill. She walked that path religiously, usually while carrying a few gallons of water on her head she retrieved from the community tank. She credits her head-strong nature to this. "Mama neva have much, enno? but she teach us fi mek due wid wha wi have. If we neva learn, we would surely dead." She had this way of referring to death as if it could occur at a moment's notice and for no good reason at all, which in actuality, she was right. "Stop drink yuh wata so fass, you gwan dead!" Or "Stop run dung di hill so fass, yuh gwan dead!!" and often "Bwoy yuh nuh tiyad fi hear seh if yuh nuh top run yuh mouth yuh ago dead?" That is to say drinking too fast will eventually lead to death, running down a steep hill too fast will lead to death and talking too much *had* to cause death. The ideas seemed irrational, but they were nothing far from the reality she had witnessed. The peaceful island of Jamaica was also home to relentless violence. The violence would then lead and become home to her dead husband who was forty years her senior. To this day, she remembers him fondly and respectfully. She still calls him "Mr. Brown."

"Missa Brown, neva ramp enno? If mi eva look pon a next man, him jealous." She discussed his jealous rage casually, explaining that a wandering eye was not permitted in her household; in fact, she was strictly punished if caught despite the fact that she was only sixteen. She found it most calming to discuss him while preparing herself for work, a job she had maintained since moving to the U.S and settling into her American home.

Her new home was quaint, and she adjusted quite nicely to running water that spurted out hot water at her convenience. Everything was simpler in America. The microwave easily heated up leftover meals, the television carried more than two working channels, and she no longer needed a "gas man" for her stove; the electric wired stove heated right up with a turn of a knob. The culture is still rich throughout her home. At first glance, it seems traditional, but traces of Jamaica are embroidered in each corner, crevice and seam. The white cabinets are typically filled with Caribbean seasoning,

including jerk sauce and turmeric.
Jamaican parables and sayings rest
in tiny frames throughout the
house. The ceilings aren't high,
but it is good enough for her. Her
favorite room was the kitchen and
its size hardly compared to what
she was used to. It stands larger
than both the kitchen and living
room of her house back home
combined, and she loves it. "Wow,
dis kitchen is so big. Mi inna

society now," she beamed when she first walked into her future home.

She loved her room too and loved to spend time there when she wasn't working. Atop of her wooden dresser were picture frames holding images of Mr. Brown. He wasn't very tall—stood about 5'7 and held a worn expression. The images reveal that he had full eyes, just as Mrs.

Brown fondly recounts. His skin was the color of mahogany and under his straight nose was an even grin. He wore a striped, neat, button up shirt and brown slacks to cover his thin legs. She was noticeably bigger than him in size, but as fate would have it, they matched. Together, they looked perfect and the differences didn't matter. She glances at them each time she prepares for work.

The talks often begin as she pulls over a short, brown-highlighted wig to mask her greased curls. She never leaves for work without it.

"Dem no like see mi hair, enno? so mi juss do wha mi affi do. Mi hair did pritty doe. Missa Brown did plat it up all di while by himself." She fondly recounts the times her husband would braid her hair before sending her off to work. He taught her how to do everything. The woman she is today is often attributed to his efforts. Now, even without his help, she manages to do all things by herself, and of course, with the help of God. As she rolls nude stockings over plump legs, she breathes heavily to fight them on, always somehow tearing them and leaving a run that would extend to her thighs before dismissing it altogether.

"Chuh, mi cyon badda. Dat gud, it can gwan." She loves Elizabeth Taylor's White Diamonds perfume. The strong scent always lingers in her room long after she leaves. Like clockwork, she presses down to release the strong aroma on her neck in two quick pumps—one spray on each side.

"Missa Brown was a proppa man. Him woulda love da cologne ya. It smell sweet." Her face subtly changes, and if you don't look close enough, you'll miss the nostalgia she creates for herself. Her phone has been ringing off the hook, but she ignores it and decides to answer it at a later time. Nothing can be that important right now, she believes.

"Alright Mrs. Brown. Yuh good to go," she says to herself while looking in the mirror, making miniscule brush-ups to her face and wig. She has never referred to herself under her maiden name, and after Mr. Brown's death, she resolved to never remarry. Instead, she relies on her Christian beliefs and her faith in God to move forward.

"Mi know seh Massa God a God." Mrs. Brown firmly believed that if God wanted her to remarry, another man as good as Mr. Brown would have come along, but because she never saw anyone that could fit his shoes, she never attempted to remarry again. She concluded that loneliness wouldn't kill her, and she'd devote the rest of her life to working hard and serving God.

Each one of her seven children would tease her.

"Mama nuh easy, enno? Mi nuh know how shi do it," her second eldest son Dinsdale would say. His bald crown is unmistakable, and his skin wears the darkest shade of brown. He's commonly referred to by his nickname, Pundu (poon-due), or BlackBoy.

"Mi nuh business wha none a yuh affi seh," she'd assert defensively. "Mi alright by miself.

"Aye sah, yuh good. Yuh good. Yuh good. Yuh good, mama. Yuh good." And just like that, the conversation would end right there. It was a constant debate. Her children never understood why she never sought another husband when The Bible says a widow could. They never understood just how she grew so contented by herself.

She'd use them to defend her reasoning, explaining that she had no use for any more children beyond the seven received with their father, so there was no point in pursuing another man. Understanding her reasoning, they could only settle upon one thing—that she is indeed *good*.

Even this day she still works, staying true to the promise she made to herself years ago. Despite the fact that 7 decades are now behind her, she presses on by maintaining the duties once demanded of her years ago. On a daily basis, she lets the steam of the iron moisten her face as she presses clothes. This always comes right before hovering above a boiling pot of food. As she kneads and forms flour dumplings in the palms of her hands, she hums his favorite song.

"Woke up dis mornin', smiled at the risin' sun. Three little birds are at my doorstep…" She begins. Bob Marley's *Everything is going to be Alright* joins the senses in the air and she smiles at each chorus. She's continues peacefully as if she's living with the idea that he's still checking up on her to ensure

she hasn't changed. She's good because she hasn't. She won't remarry even if she could. She wouldn't risk someone stealing her last name, a name she's worn with pride since her years as a Jamaican teen.

There are a distinct few that are given the opportunity to call her something else. Sometimes, she puts aside her maintained wifely duties, and assumes the role of someone her children have made her become over the years. For those like myself, Mrs. Brown lets a selected few call her—

Gramma.

"Nobody nah change mi, an nobody cyaa change mi name. A Brown mi name, an a dat mi seh. Who don't like it, bite it."

Tears

Following a small, sharp stab under the lid, he quickly lifted his index finger to meet the eye. With a loose fist dangling behind it, he pushed his finger against the irritated eyelid and rubbed. He rubbed vigorously against his closed eye. He pressed down on each corner of the eye to locate where it settled. The sharp sting tormented his eye as it sat wedged in between an unseen corner. He resolved to let his cornea rub against the masking flesh in search of the sharp sting's return.

"Whataya doing?" his wife asked through barely parted teeth. She was tired and annoyed, but so was he. He sat up in the bed and exhaled heavily. He said nothing as his frustration grew. She finally sat up and looked into his face. His eyes were still closed and all she could see were his eyeballs

gliding under his lids.

"Whataya doin?"

"I'm praying. What does it look

like I'm doin'? Somethin's stuck in

my eye."

"Well don't just sit there. Tryta get

the thing out!"

"Joanie, go back to bed."

"Well, I can't if you sittin' up

fussin about that eye."

He whipped the sheets off his legs and headed straight towards the bathroom. He leaned over the ceramic face basin to meet the mirror. His eye was red.

"Oh my God, what's that? Pink eye?" said his wife approaching him from behind.

"Joanie, go back to bed."

"Here, lemme blow it." She pursed her lips together in a small circle and exhaled quickly into his

eye.

"PHEW!"

"Ah, Joanie! C'mon, that neva

works for nobody, now!"

"Quit whining, you want it out or

not?"

She used her right hand's thumb

to lift his upper eyelid. She blew

wind into his eye again.

"Wouldya stop that, Joanie?!" he said

"Well do you still feel it?"

He closed his eyes and rolled them beneath the veiling flesh.

"I think you got— "suddenly a small prick avenged the eye.

"Dammit, it's still in there!"

"Hold still! Lemme see!" Joanie lifted the eyelid once again. She examined it carefully and bent her head to peer underneath the raised lid.

"Roll your eye to the left…now to the right."

He motioned his eye to each direction.

"Well honey, I gotta say, I don't see a thing in there."

"It's in there, Joanie."

"Well, I dunno then. You take care of it. I'm goin' back to bed."

She raised her hands, let them down dismissively, and walked back into the dark room. He shook his head and turned back to the mirror. His four fingers peeled down at his right cheek and he searched the eye again—nothing. He turned both hot and cold-water knobs protruding from the sink and washed his face aggressively. As he dried it with the face towel hanging from its rack, he peered deeply into the mirror again and still failed to spot his eye's tormentor. Suddenly, the distant sound of a wailing baby diverted his attention. He turned around swiftly and walked slowly to investigate the source. He peered into the dark room where Joan was resting.

"Joanie, you hear that?"

Her teeth kissed in annoyance.

"Hear what, Will? The sound of you wakin' me up again?"

"Ah, fugghedit" he decided and started preparing for work.

William Carson simply could not miss work again. He was too close to his promotion and he had already taken off too much time last quarter following the accident. He's been pretty strong about it, or so it seemed; he drowned himself in work after it all happened. Joan stayed home. She rarely removed her bathrobe most days, and her slightly graying hair rested shaggily upon the nape of her neck. She hadn't worked since it happened and would dress to leave the house only once a week to meet the therapist. "[She] was healing quite nicely," the therapist thought yet she never failed to question: "Now where's that husband of yours?" Joan smiled slightly each time, "Not yet Doctor. He just aint ready yet."

William simply felt he had no time to deal with "no gotdamn therapist to talk about feelings I already know I have." That didn't stop it from aging him. His hairline had begun to recede, and his dark, full eyebrows regularly furrowed together in deep discontentment. His broad shoulders over his husky frame made him appear stronger than he was. He and Joanie had reached a silent agreement to never discuss it again. Instead, she focused her attention on miniscule details of their empty house, and regularly fixated her energy on simple matters. She wasn't any taller than he was, and since it happened, she let go of the figure he once admired. As he walked outside, he briefly held the unlock button of his car's remote until he heard its apt yet welcoming jingle—boop-boop.

Both eyes watered as he drove, and he lifted his right hand to unfold the car mirror resting above him. The blinding-sun only made matters worse, and he needed to make it to work that day. His eyes squinted while flooding above his cheeks, and he raised the bridge of his shoulder to wipe the tears away.

His eyes shifted to meet the mirror that exposed all that was behind him, and that's when he saw it--Two small feet protruded from the inside of a black car seat. Resting on both sides of the seat were two carelessly unclasped straps of its fastening belt. A black SUV sped uncontrollably behind him—it was happening again. His heart thumped violently and with a quick throw of both hands over the steering wheel, he swayed the car to the highway's safe shoulder. A loud beep emerged from the small Volkswagen that had been trailing him before, and the little green car sped away. He turned to look back, and nothing nor anyone was there.

He exhaled deeply as his head dropped back. He closed his

eyes towards the car's gray, filament sky. He felt the prick in his eye again and shook his head softly. "Dammit" he whispered to himself and he involuntarily cried all the way to work.

As he parked into the first vacant space he spotted, he reached for a pair of sunglasses hidden inside of his glove compartment. He placed them on and peered through the hovering mirror before refolding it and jumping out of his car.

"Hey! Aren't we cool today?" New-exec Richard "Dick" Duggard stepped out of his way and slightly raised both hands mockingly.

"Yea, well." he said and breezed toward his office.

He knew that if he could just hide behind his office door for the day's remainder, he could not only attempt to relieve his eye, but get his work done in peace.

Knock, knock, knock

So much for that.

"Hey Carson, I barely recognized ya with those Bond shades on." Duggard asserted presumptuously.

"Just tryin' something new I guess."

"Yea well, boss wants to see ya. Somethin' about last week's reports."

Damn, he had forgotten about filing those reports. It was the third time this month.

"Alrighty, let him know I'll be right there."

"Sure thing," Duggard said while closing the door. Just before the door had a chance to close completely, Duggard stepped back in.

"Oh, and by the way, you might want to get rid of those things. He seems pretty ticked."

"Thanks, Dick" he said with a stiff smile.

"Not a problem!" The door closed.

William removed the sunglasses and buried his eyes in both palms.

He looked into the computer screen and noticed that the eye had become both red and swollen. He slightly loosened his tie from the nape of his neck and flattened his suit's jacket over his chest with sweaty palms. He walked over to Mr. Dean's office.

Knock, knock, knock

"Boss you wanted to see me?"

"Get in here, Carson," Mr. Dean said without diverting his attention from the papers in his hands. Mr. Dean was tall and carried a strong masculinity that was especially prevalent in his jawline. He was stern but fair, and the fact that his desk was always crowded with paperwork never made him one for eye-to-eye conversations.

Carson sat down nervously and held his head down.

"Look Carson, I'm not gonna be short with you. I know last quarter was tough on you, but you are still one of my best guys. I'd hate for the promotion to—what the hell is goin' on with that eye?" he said finally looking in Carson's direction.

The sharp, sting floated around the roof of his eye, but Carson still sat bravely in a feeble attempt to ignore it. Tears continued to fall from both the irritated eye and its sympathetic partner.

"Ah, it's nothin' Boss. Just got something in my eye is all."

"No, no, no. I don't want to take any chances, Carson. You go home and take the rest of the day off— "

"But Boss— "

"Now, now, go home and take it easy. Try to finish those reports from home."

He sighed digressively.

"Yes, sir." He held both arms of the chair for support, gained balance on both feet, and turned to walk away.

"Hey Carson, give Joanie my best will ya?"

"Yes, sir."

Will returned to his desk, gathered the documents he would need to review and went home.

"Joanie! I'm home!" Will yelled as he walked into the front door. He was greeted by silence.

"Joanie?" he walked down the hallway leading to his bedroom while rubbing his eye. He stopped midway when he noticed the baby's room door was wide open.

He hadn't been inside since the accident, and he couldn't help but go in. He could still smell the faint scent of Will Jr—or at least, his senses automatically called to the scent on sight of the nursery, and he walked in cautiously as if afraid to taint the aroma.

He looked at the crib that had been empty for nearly two years, and he reached for the white cotton bib with blue letters etched on its face "Daddy's Boy."

Suddenly his already flooded eyes began to pour. He sobbed violently into the bib and covered both eyes with it.

Joanie approached him from behind and held him as he wept. She swept her arms around his waist and shifted from behind him to meet his face as they both slowly fell to the ground. With streaming cheeks, she watched him sob and held him as he continued. She knew that now, he was ready.

"I should-a fast-ened that belt, Joani-eee," he said hiccupping through each word, his body shivering.

"It's okay, Will. It wasn't your fault. That man was drunk outta his mind and you know it. C'mon now we're gonna get through

this."

She was sobbing now too, and she

assured him with false confidence.

It's been almost two years and she

couldn't get in the car with him.

She couldn't bring herself to be

his passenger. Deep down, a small

part of her blamed him just the

same.

The sun was beginning to settle and a small shadow casted through the open windows of the well-lit room. Finally, his sobbing faded, and his body seemed to release what was left with an exhausted exhale. He slowly removed the bib from his eyes to admire its inscription one more time.

"Well wouldya look at that," he said through blocked nasal paths.

Through blurry eyes, he noticed something resting above the distorted blue figures. There sitting faintly, was a small, arched strand of hair.

Sub-Mom Carol

Today's entry date is September 14, Two Thousand Twenty. Please hold down button and begin recording. Thank you.

'It is now 8 a.m. Mother will be up to warn you in 5 minutes, 55 seconds. Please wake before then. (pause) It is now 8 a.m. Mother will be up to warn you in 5 minutes, 50 seconds.

Please wake before then. (pause) It is now--"

Shutt uuuup! The voice stops. She is by far the worst Christmas gift I have ever received. All the parents thought it was a good idea to buy some help—the new Sub-Mom 2020. Apple has outdone itself. I hate it. My mother constantly recollects on the old days when the only things that had touch screens were cellphones and those ancient tablets. This is not the way to keep up with the times. Damn robots are taking over as if we don't have it easy enough already. Each morning, I wake up to the voice of my Sub-Mom Carol, and before I can roll over, she's already spreading half my bed. Wait till' I wake up dammit! Mom absolutely loves her, and dad is hardly home to notice. Her built-in toaster especially gives me the creeps. Two slightly burnt slices of bread eject out of her abdomen like bills from one of those old cash registers. Why the hell would I want toast that has already been in someone's stomach? This is ridiculous. No one is thinking anymore. This obsession of over thinking is what got us in this mess in the first place.

"Shayna, wake up! Time for school!"

"5 MORE MINUTES!"

Same routine. As you know, I'm annoyed about the same thing every day. Mom and I used to be tight, but she has stepchild me ever since she started work.

20 percent remaining on voice-diary. Please connect to nearest portal.

Sheesh VD, even you're bailing on me. I wonder what life was like before technology. What did people do without hovercrafts back then? How did they live?

-Shayna

Today's entry date is September 15, Two Thousand Twenty. Please hold down button and begin recording. Thank you.

"How was school to-day, Shayna?"

I'm seriously in no mood to deal with Carol today, VD. But again, here she comes with these annoying, automated questions. And for goodness sakes! Can anyone please tell me why this pretend-woman is always lit up!? She legit Vampire glitters every time I come home. This is not some frickin' festival. Someone needs to turn that feature off. It's like Christmas every day in this place.

"How was school to-day, Shay-na? How was school to-day, Shay-na? How was school to-day, Shay-na?"

"Omgggsh, Carol! School was fine! I enjoyed myself, okay? May I have my room now?"

"What did you learn to-day, Shay-na? What did you learn to-day, Shay-na?"

Ugh! Sometimes I feel like I have to get out of here. Like, seriously—I want to jump off a sidewalk—sprain an ankle. That oughtta buy me a day in the hospital—two days tops; two days vacay away from the madness that is Sub-Mom Carol. Mom's completely delusional! Who the hell is buying this? Hellooo, I notice when you're not home, *mother.* This completely insults my intelligence. I'm not calling her mom, I'm sorry, I'm just not doin' it.

Knock, knock, knock—
"Shayna are you in there? It's me, honey."

"I'm good, mom!" *Now she chooses to come home.*

"Ok honey, pot-roast is in the oven."

"Okaaay!"

There's always a long pause after. I can hear her breathing outside my door. I know she wants to say something more, but the words don't quite come out. And just like that, her shadow disappears from underneath my doorway, and the footsteps recede down the hall. Slow footsteps emerge. The shadow is back.

"Shay-na, do you need help with your home-work? I am hap-py to ass-ist you."

I think I need a hobby, VD. An all day after school hobby.

-Shayna

Today's entry date is September 20, Two Thousand Twenty. Please hold down

button and begin recording. Thank you.

Sorry VD. I had to 180 this place. I was losing it. Cara let me stay over after *Ms. Carol* and I got into it. Well actually, I got into it with her. She kinda just stood there. Anyway, that's not the point. The point is, she was driving me up not one wall, but every damn wall you can think of. Like no kidding, my brain went up every wall and refused to come down after five days. *Sighs* but I think I'm good now. I missed my room. Cara doesn't have the same purple hover-fan in her room. And her automatic, cool-adjusting pillows aren't as plush as mine are. Yea, I kinda missed my simulated ceiling stars. Sleeping without 'em just wasn't the same. But dammit! Carol makes me hate this place. Wait a second, I hear something.

Omggsh, here we go…in five…four…three…two…

"Hi Shay-na, how was school to-day?"

If I quit goin' to school, you think she'll quit buggin' me?

-Shayna

Today's entry date is September 25, Two Thousand Twenty. Please hold down button and begin recording.

Thank you.

I really had a wretched week at school, VD. I need someone to talk to other than you. Don't get me wrong! You're great and all VD, I swear! I just wonder if you're really listening sometimes.

"Shay-na, my sys-tem de-tects that your en-er-gy levels are un-us-ually

low. What is wrong?" How does she do that? She's worse than mom.

"Nothing Carol, I'm fine."

"Shay-na, my sys-tem de-tects a change in heartbeat. You are ly-ing. What is wrong? Mom thinks I don't know she plays back every conversation Carol and I have. It's her totally obvious way of checking up on me. I must be desperate today.

"Why don't you have a seat, Carol."

Ok-ay, I am list-en-ing.

Sorry VD, this one isn't for you.

I'll let you know what happens.

Until next time.

-Shayna

Today's entry date is September 27, Two Thousand Twenty. Please hold down button and begin recording. Thank you.

Hey VD, so sorry I haven't spoken to you in awhile, but as much as I hate to admit it—talking to Carol has been pretty cool. She has all the answers. She's like Siri with lips. I've been talking to her about some things lately and I gotta say, she's the real deal.

"Hi Shay-na. How was school, today?"

"Oh, hey Carol, school went so well. The advice you gave me totally worked out!"

"I am happy to hear that, Shay-na. Tell me all about it."

After-note to self** I noticed mom stood at my doorway for a few seconds as I was talking to Carol. I think she's happy to see us getting along.

Today's entry date is September 30, Two Thousand Twenty. Please hold down button and begin recording. Thank you.

I walked into the smell of cookies, VD. Fresh baked chocolate chip cookies. Mom hasn't baked em' in ages.

Hi Shay-na. I baked you some cook-ies. How was school, to-day?

Y'know VD, I'm really startin' to dig her.

-Shayna

Today's entry date is October 2, Two Thousand Twenty. Please hold down button and begin recording. Thank you.

So, here's what's up. I have a date with Carol after school today, VD. I have this wicked science project coming up and my brain is giving up on me, so I asked Carol for help. "It's a date," she says. Gotta love her.

-Shayna

Today's entry date is October 3, Two Thousand Twenty. Please hold down button and begin recording. Thank you.

"Shayna, is that you I hear honey?"

What the hell? Mom's home. I wonder why? Hold on, VD. I hear her coming to my room.

"Hey, honey. I decided to take some time off work. I know I haven't been home much lately, and I know that must be hard on you with your father gone all the time and— "

"No sweat, mom. It's cool. Carol's here. You didn't have to do that, really."

"Are you sure, honey? I know having Carol around isn't the same as having me here but— "

"Seriously mom, chill okay. Everything's cool. Carol has everything under control."

She pauses for a moment

"Well okay, I'll be here if you need me."

I nod as she kisses my forehead.

Thank God, exit stage right, please.

Now where is Carol?

Today's entry date is October 5, Two Thousand Twenty. Please hold down button and begin recording. Thank you.

Today was awful VD. All I want to do is lie here. My teachers are freaking on me, Trevor has no idea that my existence even inhabits this earth and Cara has been "secretly" dating him. Worst kept secret ever—freakin' traitor. And to think, I wasted two good semesters with her. What the hell is wrong with the world? I officially hate people. These tears are filling my ears, and my heart feels like it's going to explode. I need Carol. I can't handle this.

"Oh God! Shayna honey, what's wrong? What happened at school? Why are you crying? Am I going to have to call— "

"Geez Mom, pop a Xanax. Just get me, Carol. I need Carol."

"Honey, I'm sure I can help you with whatever it is. Just talk to me."

"Carol! Could you please come here?!"

I can hear Carol approaching.

"Hi Shay-na, my sys-tem detects depressive energy levels. What is wrong?"

"Mom, could you please go and close the door? I need to talk to Carol."

I don't open my eyes to see her face, but she lifts her folded leg off the bed and walks away silently.

"Hey, Carol." I sit up and give her a hug.

Now-now--What is the mat-ter, sweet-heart? Mum-my is here.

I can still hear breathing at the door as it slowly creeks to a close.

Today's entry date is October 15, Two Thousand Twenty. Please hold down button and begin recording. Thank you.

Omgggsh VD, it's been forever. How ya been? I'm so sorry I haven't been coming to you lately, but Carol pretty much hammers all my problems out. I can't believe I used to consider pushing her out in the rain. I threw out one of mom's old laptop contraptions in the rain and the sparks that came out were awesome. I can't believe I almost did that to poor Carol. What else?

What else? OH! Weird! Mom still hasn't gone back to work. She's home baking and cooking and all that junk, but Carol can handle all that stuff sooo…I'm a little confused here. She keeps trying to find these bonding moments, but it's like please mom, just find a hobby. Like an all day after school hobby.

"Hi Shay-na. How was school, to-day?"

Gotta go!

-Shayna

Today's entry date is October 28, Two Thousand Twenty. Please hold down button and begin recording. Thank you.

I realize I've been treating you like a stepchild VD, so I'm going to start bringing you with me to school. A lot happens on those hovercrafts on the way home. I'll talk to you then.

-Shayna

Today's entry date is October 29, Two Thousand Twenty. Please hold down button and begin recording. Thank you.

OK! WOAH! I just heard a serious bang come from my house, VD. I'm at the door, and I'm panicking! Should I call the police! Dad's not even home.

Only mom and Carol's in there.

Okay, you know what? It's good.

Everything's okay. I'm sure Carol

can take em'. Those intruders have

come to the wrong house. My

Sub-Mom is frickin' Wonder

Woman. I'm going in.

"Hello? Mom? Carol?'

Today's entry date is October 29, Two Thousand Twenty.

Please hold down button and begin recording. Thank you.

V.D. I still can't believe it. I can't handle this. And I'm sorry that I'm sobbing like an uber-female right now, but this is serious. I'll have to start from the beginning…

Today, after we heard that loud "bang," I walked into the kitchen and the first thing I saw was my mom's back. She was hovering over Carol's lightless body like some psycho. There was no more glitter, V.D. Christmas was gone. Mom killed Santa for me again.

 I dropped my backpack to the ground right before I started to freak, and *my mother* whisked around and finally noticed I was standing behind her.

Sobbing continues

Do you know what this *faux mom*

had the nerve to ask me after she

killed Carol, V.D.?

"Oh hi, Shayna honey," she says

breathlessly while wiping sweat

from her face—all composed like

some heartless murderer. "How

was school today?"

Surviving the Chokehold

"It's too tight," she resolved as she met the grasp of a man who attempted to violently rip off her head. "He's choking me," she thinks and questions why. Either he was assisting the excruciating process the new mother just endured, or judging by his mask, he was a criminal—possibly a baby-napper. The question was asked, sometime after, in the midst of an uncomfortable discussion held with the growing mother. "Mommy's confused now," she believes, and just as quickly she silences the remaining questions that were once screaming in her head. What about—no, she thinks, and the thought is gone. She still doesn't know how she got inside the tummy to begin with, she notes, but decides to rest the conversation for a later time when her mother could take it. She has no idea she is being shielded, but for now, Barney was coming on and the questions are nearly eradicated by the joy of the purple-felt dinosaur.

Shortly after alphabet memorization, she stepped into the halls of Central High School. Health class is room 214 no, 215—she thinks, and decides to step into the space, that she now believes, was designed to tell her the truth. The real truth—*her mother is a liar*. She's not angry, "that movie she watched that summer" drops into thought. It seems, somehow, she always knew. Again, she confronts the now-experienced mother with more questions. She now knows the truth about the day she was wrangled into this world, but unfortunately, she is left with curiosity. Once again, the experienced mother is left flustered and the lying regulation-enforcer decides to abruptly leave the conversation. She watches a few more movies and listens to enough pillowed talk to know that it's all real.

After attending the baby shower of her best friend shortly after leaving the halls of her high school for the final time, she decides that she misses the day

that her conception was a mystery.

She thinks that too much

complication came with knowing,

especially for her best friend

whose growing abdomen resulted

into a series of wailing screams

only to be compared to the

sounds the new mother belted out

as the masked man proceeded to

pull. She watches in terror and

soon finds her airway is being

constricted. She returns home to the aged-mother and buries her head into her chest, hoping that her mother would save her from the chokehold yet again. She vainly hopes the lies would be exhumed and brought back to life, and that she'd be shielded once more.

Now hiding before darting eyes, she decides to share her chokehold survival using a short narrative. You finish reading it to

yourself.

I Still Remember

I still remember her, though I am certain that I'm not even a thought of her subconscious. I had never been to her house, but that didn't seem necessary at the time. Her Power Rangers lunchbox was almost identical to mine. We shared the same wooden cubby that was aligned with the rest in back of out pre-kindergarten classroom. Her blue eyes were barely exposed under thick bangs, and her pale skin made her seem cold all the time. I still remember the day she went away. The cafeteria was filled with rows of lengthy gray tables, and it smelled of stale pizza and bagels. The walls seemed blander that day as they reflected on the eggshell white painting. Indistinct conversations, paper airplanes and laughter crowded the air. I had reserved a space next to me for her as usual, and although we had argued over "who gets to be the pink ranger" the day before, I was confident that we'd hug it out like we tended to do. Her shoulder length hair was always slightly disheveled, but whenever we hugged, she smelled like the blueberry waffles I always begged my mother to buy. I still remember her small face and smaller voice. She sat next to me as usual and reached for the hug I had long anticipated. As we segregated, her blue eyes were moist and for once, fully exposed. "I'm leaving. My mommy said I have to go to a new school." My face softened at that point, and even today, almost 20 years later, I still remember her. Her name even escapes me now and I doubt I'd recognize her if we met today, but still for whatever it is worth…I

remember.

Jason

His ear-distorting gauges are what you notice first. The second is the smoke lifting from the tail of his cigarette. He doesn't notice that you're watching, but you figure its better that way. He has no regard for the cold and doesn't even consider masking his hands from it. Instead, he opts to shove one hand in his peeling, leather-resembling jacket and leave the other to deliver his nicotine fix for the morning. Jason doesn't drive much. What's the point? Everything he needs is in walking distance. You continue to peer at him over half-eaten pizza from inside the restaurant across the way. You consider offering him a slice, but you decide he'd prefer not to be bothered. He probably wouldn't accept it anyway. You've been watching him indulge in his cigarette and ignore the cold for over two minutes now. He leans on the yellow fire-hydrant behind him that is resting on the pavement, and he dismisses each vehicle as it passes by. People walk around him and ignore him just the same. He doesn't care. The fight he had with Monica the night before might make him stay out there all day. Who needs her? His dark hair is long enough to cover one eye when finger-combed towards the back. You are sipping your coke now, contemplating how long it's been. You've lost track of time. Yet somehow, it beats going home. Instead, you'll be like Jason. Leave the cares of this world in a smoldering haze. You don't smoke, but you'll learn to like it. It's all downhill when you finish the first one. Yea, who needs Monica? She probably never understood him. He can't take judgment like that all of the time. Who the heck does she think she is? A young man approaches him with an endearing hug. He flicks his third cigarette to the ground and lifts him with a warm embrace. Hand-in-hand, they walk away. You turn back to your now cold pizza and throw what's left of it in the trashcan resting nearby. You guess it's time to go home.

Awake

I don't visit the country often, and I rarely find time to assess the trees or all that nature offers—but here I am. To my surprise, and after what seemed like a long rest, I woke to find myself invading a foreign bed. I jumped suddenly as if my body could sense the difference before it had the chance to register through my senses. This room is a dull green, and noticeably absent is a television. This room, it seems, was designed to induce forced relaxation. The telephone is missing, and outside my window, acres of nature strive for miles. Where is everyone? My memory has escaped me. I don't quite remember what happened. I remember the trembling started again. While walking to work, a violent tremble emerged from my bones. The dizziness was overwhelming! Yes, I remember! —All the faces that surrounded me when my legs gave out. I'm here now. The details of what happened in between are more than a blur; they are completely out of mind. I can't believe this happened again.

"You're awake." I heard my father say. "How are you feeling?" The bed let out a slow squeak as he sat down next to me.

"Not too bad. Just a little confused is all." I pause for a moment before I ask. "Where'd you bring me this time?"

He inhaled deeply and exhaled forcefully as if the response would consume too much of his energy. "We've been telling you to take it easy for a while now, sweetheart. You're tired."

My question still remains, "Where am I, Dad?"

"When you were a little girl, you used to love the country. We'd go apple picking in early fall and finish it up with a visit to the pumpkin patch just before winter. This place is best for you."

The question is still unanswered. I suddenly jump out of bed and approach the door.

"Honey—" I can hear him say from the distance, but I'm already on a mission.

As I walk down the stairs, I'm greeted by a circle of people that is formed in what appears to be a living room area. All heads turn simultaneously to meet my face of confusion.

"Come, join us," said a calm-tone emerging from the pack. "We've been expecting you."

Family Portrait

His mother Ellen had worked as a school teacher all of his life. He couldn't help but feel that her love for "her kids" surpassed the love she had for him. "Oh honey, you'll never believe what my kids did today?" Blah, blah, blah. He grew bored of hearing it. She had this habit of providing meaningless anecdotes to serve only one purpose—

highlight insignificant feats "her kids" accomplished in one day. *Pheh, who needs her?* He thought. She always bustled in moments after he released the burden his backpack weighed on his shoulder. His mind constantly drifts and plays John Lennon to mask out the stories.

His father Jimmy was a businessman. James Sr., his grandfather, had been gone for some time now, but Jimmy hardly seems to notice. He only held conversations at home consisting of four syllables. "How was work, Dad?" he'd ask hopefully. "Mm-mm-unh-unh" Jimmy. would grunt with a dismissive wave. His father was always busy. He got that.

Little Sarah was the baby of the family who frequented books with curious eyes. She spoke only when conversations were initiated by someone else, and her little world was a place he often wished he could visit. She was a rare kind, but sporadically enough, during the least expected moments, she'd tear her eyes from its tracing motion down the open page, and look up to reveal a smile, perhaps a reminder that all was well.

And then, there was him. Jim. James Rosenbaum III. His

existence was the source of much criticism ever since he was a young child.

"Hey Rosie Rosenbaum, you wanna play?" they'd taunt.

The games were never fun.

Blaine

He was short, but his build mimicked the same frame my father carried. Dark skin covered with traces of eczema never shook his love for the spotlight. He was a dancer and life of the party, a 16-year-old with a hot temper and a love for family. His nose wasn't particularly bulbous for his face, but it was a prominent feature that stood out each time he formed silly facial expressions. His teeth were decorated with bulging pink lips that too often covered his beautifully aligned smile. His jeans were always bigger than his body could support, and his over-sized tees tended to match the caps he sported daily. On the day of his funeral, he changed his style. Always being the center of attention, he went out with a bang. His skin was flawless that day; the preserving make-up was evenly smoothened out over his face. His loose jeans were traded in for fitted black pants. A sharp button-up and black-suited jacket replaced his baggy shirt. He didn't wear his smile that day and he hasn't since. He hasn't danced at all since then either, but I suspect in years to come, I'll see the party come to life once more.

Self-Loathing Rant

Dammit! I'm two pounds heavier than I was yesterday. I used to think the scale was broken, but each time I'm forced to entertain relatives, they each rest flat feet stemming from thin bodies on it and inevitably brag about its reports. Great. We're bonding. "So, who's the lucky guy?" they proceed to ask, and then I am forced to do what any rational person in my situation would do—I shamelessly lie. His name is Jason, or whatever. I gotta get that right, they almost caught on last time. "Yea, Justin is doing well. He actually— "I was interrupted mid-story. "I thought his name was Jason, honey?" Damn. "Well-uh, Justin is a pet name I call him. He hates when I do it, but it all stems back from…" yada, yada, yada. The shameless lying continues from that point. Truth is, I haven't been on a date in two years. Only Ben & Jerry want me, and I think they're causing the rift between my scale and I. Each day, I sit on my couch and entertain them as I watch my years of school whirl quickly down a dark abyss. I call it the "drain of time wasted."

About Last Night

"I like, can't speak today. My mouth is so dry."

"Seriously, what'd you do last night?"

The question seemed easy enough, but snippets of blurred faces and lit herbs slowly crept into my memory—OH! and booze! there was definitely booze.

"I literally cannot remember, man."

It wasn't a complete lie. I don't remember exactly what I did last night. I can only remember what they did. I wonder who that girl was? What's her face? The tall brunette. I have got to find her number. She's the one face of last night I can't forget.

"Hey, I can't find my shoes. Do you know where they are? I have class in like 15 minutes," said the leggy brunette appearing from my bedroom doorway.

Oh yeeeeaaa, that's right. I DID get her number. In fact, we really bonded last night. She's a business major and her name is…well, she's a business major.

"Hang tight, I'll help you find em'."

My roommate stopped grazing over the letters of his keyboard to glance over.

"Rebecca, is it?"

"Yeah, did we meet already?"

"Sort of."

"Ha! Are these yours?!" I said triumphantly.

"Sweeet, thanks!

"Sure thing."

"Ugh!" she grunted after planting the end of her flawless stems into her shoes. "I seriously cannot handle heels when I'm sober."

"I'll call you."

"Cool, see you around."

The door closes behind her after she stumbles across the marble floor.

"Dude, seriously. You have got to stop smoking."

"I know," I say. My mouth is still too dry and my memory still too faded. Maybe I will call her back, but right now, I need something more.

"Cheetos and soda are in the fridge," he said.

The greatest. He always knows.

8 A.M.

I have one last strand of sanity directly linked to one last nerve, which my boss happily dances on each time I punch in. Every morning, the clock reads 8 AM. I'm here faithfully and on time, yet I'm still treated as an intern, never mind the fact that my ideas are genius. I only have a Master's in Graphic Design. Now I'm the dork that attends dinner parties just to recite a dying refrain that inevitably sends me home by myself. "Hi, I'm a technician for AOL." I mean, seriously, who uses AOL anymore? I mean, for anything?

How did I end up here? I'm supposed to be working for Disney right now, dammit.

Ugh, it reeks of donuts and bad attitudes in here, and my cubicle is growing smaller and smaller. It's too tight in here. *Ring, ring* "*hello, AOL*" pause "*I'm sorry, my department can not sufficiently help you with your difficulties. I'll transfer you over to our technician.*" –Clockwork. They all send 'em to me. Jerks.

They know when I'm taking my informal breaks; our cubicles are separated by thin gray walls. I can't take this place. Stupid stapler. Stupid copier. Stupid boss. Stupid job.

"Get back to work, Johnson."

Damn, he's caught me job-loathing again. I think he senses when I'm going off to that place. He breezes back to his office haughtily and closes the door. Is that music? I know I hear music. That man is in there dancing on my last nerve. He cannot treat me like this. That's it, I'm done. I'm walking right out of here and I'm calling human resources. I—

Johnson? —am—*Johnson?* —done wasting my—*JOHNSON!*

I snap out of it.

"What are you doing here? Didn't you get off like 20 minutes ago?" said what's-her-face with the glasses from Customer Service.

I hastily gather my day's reports and throw them in my briefcase. I find that investing energy into hating my job kills the time. Before I know it, it's 4 P.M.

As I step outside and feel the cool breeze on my face, I inhale deeply and embrace the moment.

Ah, another day's work completed, and I'm that much closer to retirement. I'm that much closer to fishing trips, traveling and landing Gisele Bundchen. *"Hi, my name is Kyle Johnson. I'm a retired graphic designer for Disney. May I take you out sometime?"* She'll wrap her Brazilian arms around me, and I'd die while in my prime.

This place isn't a bad start. It's definitely a resume booster. Nope, Disney won't turn me down after this.

Yep, *I think I love my job.*

Well, that is…until tomorrow at 8 A.M.

www.ingramcontent.com/pod-product-compliance
Lightning Source LLC
Chambersburg PA
CBHW051651040426
42446CB00009B/1078